THE STORY OF GISÈLE PÉLICOT

How One Woman's Courage Exposed the Dark Realities of Abuse & Transformed the Fight for Victims' Rights in France

Laura D. Everett

All rights reserved. No part of this publication may be reproduced, distributed, or transmitted in any form or by any means, including photocopying, recording, or other electronic or mechanical methods, without the prior written permission of the publisher, except in the case of brief quotations embodied in critical reviews and certain other noncommercial uses permitted by copyright law.

Copyright © 2024 by Laura D. Everett

Table of Content

Introduction	**6**
Chapter 1	**8**
The Early Life of Gisèle Pélicot	8
Education and Aspirations	11
Chapter 2	**16**
Family and Marriage	16
The Hidden Darkness	19
Family Dynamics	22
Chapter 3	**25**
The Years of Abuse - A Nightmare Unseen	25
The Scope of the Abuse	28
The Unknowing Victim	31
Chapter 4	**34**
Discovery and Revelation	34
The Police Investigation	34
Gisèle's Awakening	37
A Public Decision: Waiving Anonymity	40
Chapter 5	**43**
The Legal Battle	43
The Men Involved: Who They Were	46
Trials and Tribulations	49

Chapter 6 — 53
- The Social and Legal Implications — 53
- Public Outrage and Advocacy — 57
- Media Coverage and Public Perception — 61

Chapter 7 — 66
- Gisèle's Resilience - A Survivor's Journey — 66
- Facing the World: Becoming an Advocate — 70
- The Long Road to Healing — 74

Chapter 8 — 79
- Current Challenges and Her Role Today — 79
- Gisèle's Present-Day Life — 83
- Challenges of Advocacy — 87

Chapter 9 — 91
- The Global Impact of Gisèle Pélicot's Story — 91
- The Broader Conversation on Sexual Violence — 94
- Changing Attitudes and Policies — 98

Conclusion — 103
- The Road Ahead - Gisèle Pélicot's Legacy — 103
- The Legacy of Courage — 107
- Gisèle's Message to the World — 111

Introduction

Gisèle Pélicot's story is one that both devastates and inspires. For nearly a decade, she lived a life shrouded in darkness, unaware of the monstrous betrayal orchestrated by her own husband. Drugged and abused by over 50 men without her knowledge, her life became a nightmare she never knew she was living. The sheer magnitude of this betrayal, discovered through thousands of images and videos stored on her husband's computer, is almost too difficult to comprehend. Yet, amidst this harrowing discovery, Gisèle made a decision that would change the narrative, she chose to fight back.

In a world where victims often retreat in silence, Gisèle stood tall. Waving her anonymity, she faced her abusers and the world, not as a broken woman but as a beacon of resilience. Her bravery sparked public outrage and ignited discussions around sexual violence, consent, and the justice system's failings.

This book seeks to capture not only the brutal reality of Gisèle's experience but also the strength it takes to survive such trauma. Her journey reminds us that even in the darkest moments, courage and dignity can rise from the ashes. Gisèle Pélicot is not just a victim, she is a symbol of resilience, justice, and hope.

Chapter 1

The Early Life of Gisèle Pélicot

Childhood and Family Origins

Gisèle Pélicot's story, though marked by tragedy in her later years, began like many others, with a foundation rooted in family and community. Born into a modest, close-knit family in a small village in France, Gisèle's childhood was shaped by traditional values, a strong sense of family duty, and the culture that surrounded her. The village she grew up in was one of those picturesque French settings, where the rhythm of life was dictated by seasons, markets, and the quiet hum of community life. Her family, though not wealthy, was well respected within their small community. They worked hard, celebrated their joys together, and leaned on each other in times of difficulty.

Gisèle's parents were hardworking individuals. Her father was a farmer, a man of few words, but his dedication to providing for his family spoke volumes. He taught her the value of hard work and perseverance, qualities that would later become essential in her life. Her mother, on the other hand, was the emotional center of the family. She managed their home with care, ensuring that Gisèle and her siblings were raised with love, discipline, and an unwavering sense of right and wrong. It was from her mother that Gisèle learned the importance of resilience, a lesson that would become crucial as the storm clouds of her future began to gather.

Growing up, Gisèle was a bright and curious child, always eager to learn from the world around her. She spent her days running through the fields, playing with her siblings, and listening to the stories of the elders in her community. These stories, often tales of hardship and survival, would later serve as a quiet reminder of the strength she would need to navigate her own unimaginable trials.

The community played a large role in shaping Gisèle's early years. In her village, everyone knew one another, and it was common for neighbors to look out for each other's children. This sense of communal protection created a cocoon of safety around her as she grew up. She was often seen as a gentle, kind girl who showed empathy for others, traits that endeared her to both her peers and adults alike.

As a child, Gisèle was fascinated by the world beyond her village. She would often dream about the future, imagining a life filled with possibilities that extended beyond the confines of her rural surroundings. Her father, though traditional, encouraged her education, believing that his daughter could one day break free from the limitations of their small world. But her mother, while supportive, also reminded her that family and community were the bedrock of life, a lesson Gisèle held close, even as she dreamed of more.

The cultural backdrop of Gisèle's childhood was deeply influenced by French traditions. Festivals and religious celebrations were integral to her upbringing, grounding her in a sense of belonging that stretched beyond the immediate family unit. These traditions, often centered on community gatherings, provided her with a deep sense of identity and pride. The village may have been small, but the richness of its culture offered a wide lens through which Gisèle began to view the world.

Education and Aspirations

Education was a significant part of Gisèle's life from an early age. Unlike many girls of her generation who were often discouraged from pursuing academic goals, Gisèle's parents believed in the power of education. Her father, in particular, saw it as the key to a better life for his children, and he made sure that Gisèle had access to the best schooling available within their means. From her first day at the village school, it was clear that she had a natural thirst for knowledge. She excelled in her studies, often coming home with high marks and praise from her teachers.

Gisèle's academic prowess quickly became a source of pride for her family. As she grew older, her teachers began to recognise her potential, encouraging her to think beyond the village and pursue further education in one of France's larger cities. For Gisèle, this prospect was both thrilling and terrifying. On one hand, she yearned for the opportunity to explore the world beyond the familiar boundaries of her rural upbringing. On the other hand, the idea of leaving behind the safety and comfort of her home, family, and community was daunting.

By the time she reached secondary school, Gisèle had developed a clear vision for her future. She dreamed of becoming a teacher, believing that education could be her way of giving back to the world. She had been deeply inspired by her own teachers, who had opened her eyes to the possibilities of a life enriched by learning. For Gisèle, teaching was not just a profession; it was a calling. She imagined herself standing in front of a classroom, guiding young minds, helping them to discover the same joy in learning that had defined her own academic journey.

However, as with many dreams, the path to realization was not straightforward. The financial strain of further education weighed heavily on her family, and while her father was determined to support her aspirations, the realities of their economic situation made it difficult. Still, Gisèle remained undeterred. She began taking on small jobs during her school breaks, saving every penny in the hope that one day she would be able to attend university. Her resilience during this time was remarkable; despite the obstacles in her way, she refused to let go of her ambitions.

In addition to her academic aspirations, Gisèle was also deeply influenced by the cultural and social movements of her time. France was undergoing significant changes during her formative years, and she was keenly aware of the shifting dynamics in society. The feminist movements that were gaining momentum across Europe sparked her interest, and she began to see her own aspirations as part of a larger fight for women's rights and equality. She believed that by pursuing her education and career, she could contribute to the progress of women in society.

As she moved closer to adulthood, Gisèle's dreams of becoming a teacher became more tangible. She continued to work hard, both academically and in her part-time jobs, slowly inching her way towards her goal. Little did she know, however, that life had other plans for her. Despite her best efforts to build a future filled with promise and opportunity, the dark events that would soon unfold in her life would change the course of her journey in ways she could never have imagined.

Chapter 2

Family and Marriage

Meeting Dominique Pélicot

Gisèle Pélicot's life, much like any other, was marked by a series of pivotal moments that defined her path, and meeting Dominique Pélicot was one of those moments. They met in what seemed like the most ordinary of circumstances, a social gathering in her hometown that brought people together. Dominique was charming, articulate, and appeared to share many of the same values that Gisèle held dear-family, commitment, and a seemingly deep respect for traditional values. He was a man of solid stature, a figure who commanded attention without being ostentatious. At the time, there was nothing to suggest the horrors that lay beneath his composed exterior.

Their courtship was, by all appearances, idyllic. Dominique swept Gisèle off her feet with his attention, affection, and promises of a life filled with stability and love. To a woman who had spent her life deeply rooted in the values of community and family, Dominique seemed like the perfect partner. He was the kind of man who would offer her the security she had always dreamed of, a partner with whom she could build a life, a family, and a future. Their romance unfolded naturally, with Dominique often making gestures that reflected his interest in both her well-being and her dreams. To Gisèle, this felt like the beginning of a perfect life.

Not long after, Dominique proposed. Gisèle, caught up in the whirlwind of love and the vision of a stable family life, agreed without hesitation. The wedding was a small but beautiful affair, filled with the warm smiles and well-wishes of family and friends. To the outside world, they were the perfect couple, two individuals who had found each other in a world filled with uncertainty, ready to face the future together. Their marriage, at least on the surface, was a union built on mutual respect and love, and for a time, it seemed that nothing could disrupt this harmonious life.

Their early years together were marked by the typical milestones of marriage, setting up a home, planning a future, and dreaming of building a family. Gisèle felt content in the life they were creating, confident that she had found a partner who would support her through life's challenges. Dominique, outwardly, was the caring husband, seemingly invested in their shared life. They spent weekends visiting family, attending community events, and hosting friends, with Dominique always presenting himself as a gracious and loving partner.

But, as we now know, the surface rarely tells the whole story. What Gisèle could not have known then, was that beneath Dominique's composed exterior lay a darkness that would unravel the very foundation of their marriage.

The Hidden Darkness

The early years of Gisèle and Dominique's marriage were, to all outward appearances, uneventful. They were what anyone would call a typical couple navigating the early stages of building a life together. Gisèle often reminisced about these years, remembering Dominique as a calm and collected man who seemed to enjoy the simple pleasures of life. He was attentive, though perhaps more reserved than one might expect from a newlywed. Still, there was no reason for Gisèle to believe that anything was amiss.

In fact, from Gisèle's perspective, the quietness of their life together was comforting. Dominique's steady nature made her feel secure, and they fell into a comfortable routine. Gisèle managed the home while Dominique worked, and on weekends they would spend time with friends and family, often hosting small gatherings at their house. The early years were full of laughter, shared meals, and long conversations about their future, which included plans for children and dreams of retirement in the French countryside.

Yet, as the years went on, there were subtle changes. Dominique, once attentive and communicative, began to withdraw. He became more secretive, spending long hours locked in his office, claiming to be overwhelmed with work. Initially, Gisèle didn't think much of it after all, Dominique had a demanding job, and she respected his need for space. But as time passed, his behavior grew more concerning. He started avoiding social gatherings, isolating himself from the family and friends they had once entertained so often. When asked about his sudden reclusiveness, Dominique would brush it off, citing stress or fatigue.

There were no immediate red flags, no glaring warning signs that screamed of the horrors that were unfolding behind closed doors. Dominique's growing coldness was concerning, but Gisèle, ever the patient and loving wife, believed that with time, things would return to normal. She thought he might be going through a rough patch, perhaps a mid-life crisis. Her friends, noticing the shift in their relationship, would ask her if everything was alright, but Gisèle always responded with a smile, convinced that her husband's behavior was just a phase.

However, there were moments when Gisèle couldn't shake the feeling that something was deeply wrong. Dominique's secretive nature began to extend to other parts of their life. He became overly protective of his phone, his laptop, and his personal space. The once open lines of communication between them were now stifled by Dominique's increasingly defensive responses. Whenever Gisèle would gently ask what was bothering him, he would either snap at her or shut down the conversation entirely.

Gisèle, with her gentle and trusting nature, didn't press further. She believed in giving Dominique the space he needed, trusting that his issues would resolve with time. Little did she know that this hidden darkness was far more insidious than she could have ever imagined. Dominique was not simply withdrawing due to stress he was concealing a monstrous double life that would soon come crashing down, leaving Gisèle devastated and betrayed in ways she couldn't have fathomed.

Family Dynamics

Family played a central role in Gisèle's life, both before and after she married Dominique. Her close relationship with her parents and siblings remained intact, even as she settled into married life. They visited often, and Gisèle was always eager to keep them involved in her life, holding on to the warmth and security of her family ties. Her parents, proud of the life she had built with Dominique, had no idea of the cracks that were slowly forming in their daughter's seemingly perfect marriage.

Her social circle, too, was supportive. Gisèle had friends from her school years who would visit and share meals, and she enjoyed the camaraderie of their gatherings. Dominique, however, had begun to distance himself from these interactions. At first, Gisèle brushed off his reluctance to join their gatherings, assuming he was simply tired or uninterested. But as his absence became more frequent, her friends began to notice.

Gisèle often found herself making excuses for Dominique's growing absence, both physically and emotionally. Her friends, sensing that something was wrong, gently encouraged her to speak about it, but Gisèle remained hopeful that things would improve. In her heart, she still believed in the man she had married, the man who had promised her a life of love and partnership.

What Gisèle didn't realize was that Dominique's distance was not simply a result of marital stress, but rather a conscious effort to hide the horrors he was orchestrating behind closed doors. The very people Gisèle had trusted family, friends, and her husband were about to become part of a nightmare that would change the course of her life forever.

Chapter 3

The Years of Abuse – A Nightmare Unseen

The Start of the Ordeal (2011)

The beginning of Gisèle Pélicot's nightmare was marked by an innocence so profound that it almost seems unimaginable in retrospect. In 2011, what seemed like an ordinary year in Gisèle's life was, in fact, the moment her world began to unravel, although she would not come to realize this for nearly a decade. This was the year when Dominique, the man she had trusted and built a life with, began systematically betraying her in the most grotesque way possible.

It all began in small, almost imperceptible steps. Gisèle had noticed that she sometimes woke up feeling groggy or disoriented, but like most people, she attributed it to the natural fatigue of daily life. Dominique, ever the attentive husband on the surface, would reassure her that she was simply overworked or perhaps under the weather. He would offer her something to help her relax, usually a drink or a pill, something he claimed was meant to ease her stress. There was no reason for Gisèle to doubt him; after all, they had been together for years, and her trust in him was unwavering.

What Gisèle did not know was that these seemingly innocent offerings were laced with sedatives, strong enough to render her unconscious for hours. Dominique, whose manipulative and controlling tendencies had deepened over the years, was now systematically drugging his wife. Each time she drank from the cup he offered or took the pill he provided, she unknowingly opened the door to the monstrous events that would follow.

Once Gisèle was unconscious, Dominique would begin his orchestrations. His role in her abuse was not passive; it was calculated, cold, and horrifyingly deliberate. He not only drugged her but facilitated her sexual assault by multiple men, over and over again. The extent of his betrayal was unimaginable, but at the time, Gisèle remained blissfully unaware of the horrors being perpetrated against her.

Dominique's control over these situations was absolute. He meticulously planned each event, carefully choosing the men who would participate in the abuse. To him, this was not a moment of emotional breakdown or temporary madness—it was an organised and ongoing violation that he maintained with disturbing regularity. The house, their home, became the scene of unspeakable crimes while Gisèle slept, completely unaware of the nightmare unfolding around her.

The start of this ordeal in 2011 marked the beginning of what would become nearly a decade of unimaginable cruelty. Yet, for Gisèle, life continued as normal. She still viewed her husband as the man she had married, a man who, while distant at times, was never a cause for deep suspicion. Little did she know, she was living in the shadow of a monster, one who had carefully crafted an illusion of normalcy while destroying the very essence of her being behind her back.

The Scope of the Abuse

As the years passed, Dominique's abuse of Gisèle grew bolder, more frequent, and more organized. What started as isolated instances of drugging and assault escalated into a horrifying operation involving dozens of men. Dominique had taken his violation of Gisèle to an almost industrial scale, systematically allowing over 50 men to assault her while she lay unconscious, completely unaware of the heinous acts being committed against her body.

Dominique's ability to carry out these crimes relied heavily on his use of drugs. He became adept at mixing powerful sedatives into her food and drinks, ensuring that Gisèle remained unconscious for long periods of time. The drugs were so effective that even if Gisèle stirred briefly, she was never fully aware of what was happening to her. Her body was present, but her mind was far from the atrocities being committed against her. Each time, Dominique reassured her that her tiredness and disorientation were nothing out of the ordinary, using his calm demeanor to mask his guilt.

The abuse did not stop at merely allowing others to assault her. Dominique took it further by documenting everything. Using hidden cameras, he recorded countless hours of footage, capturing the assaults from different angles. For him, this was not just an act of betrayal, it was a meticulously recorded operation, with each violation captured on video and stored away. He amassed a collection of thousands of images and videos, each one a testament to the grotesque betrayal of his wife's trust.

These recordings were not just for his own viewing. Dominique shared them with others in dark corners of the internet, where like-minded individuals indulged in these sickening acts. He created a network of men who participated in the abuse, carefully coordinating times and ensuring that every assault was documented. To them, Gisèle was nothing more than a body to be violated, her humanity stripped away by the very man who had vowed to protect her.

The sheer scale of the abuse is difficult to fathom. Over the years, Dominique invited over 50 men to assault Gisèle, some of them returning multiple times. These men, some of whom were strangers and others acquaintances, participated in the assaults without ever questioning the morality of what they were doing. They knew Gisèle was drugged and unaware, yet they took part in the violations without remorse.

The fact that this went on for so many years, in the comfort of her own home, adds another layer of horror to Gisèle's story. Every room, every corner of her house became a place of violation, and yet she continued to live in that space, completely unaware. What should have been a sanctuary was instead the site of her systematic abuse, filmed and shared with people she had never met.

The Unknowing Victim

Throughout these years, Gisèle lived her life in what can only be described as a tragic state of ignorance. She had no reason to suspect that her husband, the man she had chosen to share her life with, was orchestrating such horrors. Her days were spent in routine, filled with the normalcy of work, family, and the small joys that life brings. She laughed, she loved, and she continued to trust Dominique, never once suspecting that he was betraying her in the most despicable way imaginable.

The emotional toll of this deception is almost too great to comprehend. To live each day unaware of such profound abuse is a violation of the soul, not just the body. Gisèle's trust in Dominique, the foundation of their marriage, was shattered without her knowledge. Each day that passed deepened the betrayal, yet she remained blissfully unaware, living a life of quiet normalcy, while the man she trusted was methodically destroying her.

Gisèle's mental state during these years was, understandably, one of slight confusion. She often felt disoriented and fatigued, but these feelings were easily attributed to the stresses of life. Dominique had become distant, but Gisèle accepted his explanation that work was overwhelming. There was no reason for her to suspect that her weariness was the result of being drugged, or that her husband's emotional distance was the result of a double life filled with orchestrated assaults and secret recordings.

Even as friends and family began to notice subtle changes in Gisèle's demeanor, there was no obvious cause for concern. She was still the same kind, gentle woman they had always known, albeit a bit more tired, perhaps a little more withdrawn. But Gisèle herself had no idea of the monstrous crimes that were being carried out against her behind the scenes. She lived in a cruel, constructed reality, a life built on lies that would eventually come crashing down.

The realization of what had been happening to her, when it finally came, would shatter Gisèle in ways that are hard to imagine. To wake up one day and learn that the person you trusted most had orchestrated years of sexual violence against you is a cruelty beyond words. But for now, during these years, Gisèle remained the unknowing victim, a woman whose life had been stolen from her without her knowledge.

Chapter 4

Discovery and Revelation

The Police Investigation

The unraveling of the horrors committed against Gisèle Pélicot began not as a direct investigation into her personal life, but rather as part of a separate police operation. Dominique Pélicot, though seemingly a man of no particular notoriety, had drawn the attention of law enforcement for unrelated matters. It was through this investigation, as authorities sifted through Dominique's electronic devices, that they stumbled upon something far more disturbing than they had anticipated evidence of unimaginable abuse.

During a routine inspection of Dominique's computer, officers were shocked to find a trove of files that contained thousands of videos and images.

What they uncovered was a vast archive documenting years of sexual assaults committed against Gisèle while she was drugged and unconscious. The evidence, meticulously cataloged and stored, was staggering in both its volume and the sickening detail it revealed. For the investigators, what began as a minor inquiry into Dominique's activities quickly turned into a full-scale criminal investigation of sexual abuse on a massive scale.

The discovery of this digital archive was nothing short of horrifying. It wasn't just a few isolated incidents; it was a systematic pattern of abuse that had been ongoing for nearly a decade. There were thousands of images and videos, all meticulously documented and organized by Dominique. Each file told the story of a woman, unaware and defenseless, being repeatedly assaulted by numerous men. The sheer scale of the abuse was almost too difficult to comprehend.

The police immediately realized that this was no ordinary case. The level of premeditation and cruelty involved required swift action. Dominique was promptly arrested, and the authorities began piecing together the extent of his crimes. As they delved deeper into the files, they identified dozens of men who had participated in the assaults, captured in the recordings that Dominique had so carefully orchestrated. Each piece of evidence painted a grim picture of the years-long nightmare that Gisèle had unknowingly endured.

For the police, the challenge was not only in cataloging the evidence but also in preparing for the monumental legal case that would follow. Dominique had not only committed these atrocities but had also carefully documented every detail, which, in a cruel twist, became the very evidence that would condemn him. What started as a routine investigation had quickly transformed into a case of one of the most heinous betrayals imaginable—one that would soon shake the very foundations of Gisèle's life.

Gisèle's Awakening

The day Gisèle Pélicot learned the truth was the day her world came crashing down. It was not a gentle unveiling or a gradual understanding, it was a brutal, shattering revelation delivered by the very authorities who had uncovered the crimes. For years, Gisèle had lived her life without suspicion, trusting her husband, unaware that her body had been violated in the most grotesque ways imaginable while she slept, drugged and defenseless. The moment the police revealed to her the extent of Dominique's betrayal was nothing short of devastating.

Gisèle had always seen herself as a rational, composed woman. She had lived a life rooted in family, tradition, and love, values that had shaped her understanding of the world. To be told, in one crushing moment, that everything she thought she knew about her marriage, her home, and her life had been a lie was more than she could bear. The police showed her evidence, images and videos proof of what had been happening behind her back for nearly a decade. It was incomprehensible, a nightmare beyond anything she could have ever imagined.

Her first reaction was disbelief. How could this be true? How could the man she had loved and trusted be capable of such monstrous acts? Gisèle's mind raced as she tried to piece together how her life, the life she had so carefully built, had been shattered without her knowledge. But the evidence was undeniable, and slowly, painfully, the reality set in. Dominique had drugged her, violated her trust, and allowed countless men to assault her all while she remained oblivious.

The emotional toll of this revelation was immediate and profound. Gisèle's world, once filled with certainty, was now a landscape of betrayal, violation, and disbelief. She felt as though she had been living in a cruel illusion, a life constructed on lies. The psychological impact was almost too much to bear, she experienced waves of grief, rage, and humiliation. Her sense of self, her identity as a woman, had been ripped apart in an instant. She had been reduced to an object in her own home, her body used and abused without her consent.

In the weeks that followed, Gisèle struggled to come to terms with the enormity of the betrayal. She oscillated between overwhelming grief and a numb, disbelieving detachment. The woman she had been, the life she had lived, was gone, replaced by the grim reality of the nightmare that had been unfolding for years, right under her nose. The emotional and psychological scars from this revelation would be deep and lasting, marking the beginning of a long and painful journey toward healing.

A Public Decision: Waiving Anonymity

In the wake of the shocking revelations, Gisèle Pélicot was faced with a difficult choice whether to remain anonymous, as many victims of sexual abuse do, or to step into the public eye and claim her story. For many survivors, the prospect of public exposure is too painful, the stigma and shame too great. But for Gisèle, anonymity was not an option. Despite the unimaginable trauma she had endured, she made the bold and courageous decision to waive her right to anonymity. She wanted the world to know her story, to see her not as a victim, but as a survivor.

Waving her anonymity was not just a personal decision; it was a powerful statement. By choosing to reveal her identity, Gisèle took control of the narrative. She refused to be defined by the crimes committed against her, instead reclaiming her voice and her agency. For her, this was a necessary step in her journey toward healing. To remain silent, to hide in the shadows, would be to let her abusers win. But by stepping into the light, Gisèle sent a clear message: she would not be silenced, and her story would not be hidden.

This decision had profound implications, not just for Gisèle but for the wider public. By coming forward, she helped shift the conversation around sexual abuse, challenging the stigma that so often surrounds survivors. She became a symbol of resilience, showing that even in the face of unimaginable betrayal, it is possible to reclaim one's dignity and voice. Her bravery inspired others, giving them the strength to confront their own experiences of abuse and to seek justice.

Gisèle's public decision also brought much-needed attention to the systemic issues that allowed such crimes to go unnoticed for so long. Her story sparked a national conversation about the need for better protections for victims, legal reforms, and more stringent punishments for perpetrators. By revealing her identity, Gisèle turned her personal tragedy into a catalyst for change, ensuring that her story would not be forgotten, and that her suffering would not be in vain.

In the end, Gisèle's decision to waive her anonymity was an act of courage, a defiant stand against the forces that sought to destroy her. It was a powerful reminder that, even in the darkest of circumstances, there is strength in reclaiming one's narrative and using it to bring about positive change.

Chapter 5

The Legal Battle

Dominique Pélicot's Arrest

The day Dominique Pélicot was arrested marked the beginning of a complex and grueling legal battle that would expose the horrifying scope of his crimes and the lengths to which he had gone to cover them up. After the police uncovered the vast trove of images and videos documenting years of sexual assaults on his wife, Gisèle, Dominique's arrest was swift and decisive. It was a moment that brought a sense of relief to law enforcement, but for Gisèle, it was the start of a harrowing journey through the legal system.

When Dominique was taken into custody, the charges brought against him were extensive and severe. He was charged with multiple counts of aggravated rape, sexual assault, and violation of privacy, among other charges related to the systematic drugging and exploitation of his wife. The evidence was overwhelming. The thousands of images and videos found on his devices were more than enough to establish a pattern of premeditated, long-term abuse. But what made this case particularly complex was the involvement of dozens of other men who had participated in the assaults. Dominique was not acting alone, and this fact added layers of legal complexity that would take years to untangle.

As the investigation deepened, it became clear that Dominique had created a well-organized network of individuals who took part in the abuse of Gisèle. These men had been invited into Dominique's home under the guise of secrecy, knowing that Gisèle was being drugged and violated without her knowledge. The legal ramifications of this network were immense. Each of the men who participated was now implicated in a series of criminal acts, ranging from rape to conspiracy to commit sexual assault.

The arrest of Dominique marked the first step in a long and arduous legal process. The prosecution had to navigate not only the extensive evidence but also the challenge of prosecuting a case that involved multiple defendants, each with varying degrees of culpability. The legal system, often slow and methodical, now had to contend with the sheer volume of the crimes committed and the intricate web of individuals involved. This would not be a simple case of one man's guilt but a far-reaching investigation into a network of predators, all coordinated by Dominique Pélicot.

For Gisèle, the arrest of her husband was a moment of profound shock and betrayal. The man she had loved and trusted had been living a double life, orchestrating her abuse while pretending to be her protector. His arrest was not just a legal matter, it was the unraveling of her entire reality. While the justice system began to move forward, Gisèle was left to grapple with the emotional devastation of knowing that the man she had built her life with was capable of such monstrous acts.

The Men Involved: Who They Were

The involvement of over 50 men in the abuse of Gisèle Pélicot added an even more horrifying dimension to an already devastating case. These men, some of whom were strangers and others acquaintances of Dominique, willingly participated in the sexual assault of a woman who was unconscious and defenseless. The sheer number of individuals involved in these crimes was staggering, and identifying and prosecuting them would become one of the most challenging aspects of the case.

The men who participated in the abuse came from various walks of life. Some were known to Dominique through social or professional circles, while others were part of an underground network of individuals who shared a perverse interest in sexual exploitation. Each man who entered Dominique's home did so knowing full well that Gisèle was being drugged and that she had no knowledge or consent to what was happening. For them, the abuse was an act of opportunism, facilitated by Dominique's willingness to offer his wife as an object for their exploitation.

As investigators delved into the evidence, they were able to identify many of these men through the recordings that Dominique had so meticulously kept. Faces, voices, and even physical identifiers like tattoos or birthmarks helped law enforcement build a profile of each individual involved. Many of these men had no prior criminal records, making their participation in these heinous acts even more shocking. They came from all walks of life, blue-collar workers, professionals, even family men who, on the surface, led respectable lives.

The process of bringing these men to justice was painstaking. Each had to be tracked down, arrested, and questioned about their involvement. Some denied the charges, while others confessed, expressing remorse or claiming ignorance about the full extent of Dominique's manipulation. However, the evidence was damning, and there was little room for denial. The videos showed each man in the act, and their participation was undeniable.

For Gisèle, the knowledge that so many men had taken part in her abuse was a crushing blow. These were not faceless strangers, they were men who had entered her home, violated her body, and left without a trace of remorse. The betrayal she felt was compounded by the sheer number of individuals who had conspired to rob her of her dignity and bodily autonomy. As each man was identified and brought to justice, the scope of her violation became ever more apparent, deepening the psychological wounds she would carry for the rest of her life.

Trials and Tribulations

The courtroom battles that followed Dominique Pélicot's arrest were fraught with complexity, emotion, and legal intricacies. With dozens of men implicated in the abuse, the case became one of the largest and most challenging criminal prosecutions in recent memory. For the prosecution, the evidence was overwhelming but managing such a vast amount of information, coordinating between multiple defendants, and ensuring justice for Gisèle proved to be an arduous process.

The legal strategies employed by the defense were as varied as the individuals involved. Some of the men argued that they had been unaware of the full extent of Dominique's manipulation, claiming they did not know Gisèle had been drugged. Others attempted to deflect blame, suggesting that Dominique had coerced them into participating. Dominique's own defense was built on a web of deceit and denial, with his legal team attempting to cast doubt on the prosecution's evidence, despite the mountain of digital records proving his guilt.

The prosecution, however, remained resolute. The video footage, the testimonies of law enforcement, and the detailed evidence collected from Dominique's home and devices left little room for doubt. As the trial progressed, the weight of the evidence began to crush any defense the perpetrators had mounted. The men involved were not just passive participants, they had knowingly and repeatedly violated a woman who had no power to resist.

For Gisèle, the trial was an emotional rollercoaster. Each day in court was a painful reminder of the horrors she had endured. She had to relive the nightmare, listening to the details of the abuse and seeing the men who had violated her. The psychological toll was immense, as she grappled with the public exposure of her trauma while trying to find a path toward healing.

The role of evidence in the trial was crucial, but it also posed significant challenges. The sheer volume of digital records made the case slow-moving, and the legal team had to navigate a minefield of privacy laws, digital forensics, and the defense's attempts to suppress key pieces of evidence. Every video, every image, was a testament to Dominique's cruelty and the complicity of the men who participated. But each one was also a painful reminder to Gisèle of the life she had lost.

The legal complexities of the case, combined with the emotional weight carried by Gisèle, made the courtroom battles some of the most difficult moments in her journey toward justice. But through it all, she remained strong, determined to see her abusers brought to justice. In the end, the strength of the evidence and the persistence of the prosecution ensured that Dominique and the men who participated in the abuse were held accountable. But for Gisèle, the scars of this trial both emotional and psychological, would last a lifetime.

Chapter 6

The Social and Legal Implications

Legal Gaps Exposed

Gisèle Pélicot's case shook France to its core, not only because of the unimaginable cruelty she endured but also because it revealed glaring gaps in the legal framework meant to protect victims of sexual violence. As the details of the case unfolded, it became painfully clear that the law had failed to protect Gisèle for nearly a decade. These failures highlighted systemic problems within the judicial and legislative systems, particularly around the issues of sexual abuse, drug-facilitated crimes, and privacy rights.

One of the most alarming gaps exposed by this case was how easily Dominique Pélicot was able to drug and violate his wife without detection for so long. The use of drugs to incapacitate victims is not a new tactic in cases of sexual assault, but Gisèle's case underscored how difficult it is to prosecute such crimes. In many legal systems, drug-facilitated sexual assault falls into a grey area because the victim is often unaware that a crime has been committed until much later if at all. In Gisèle's case, she did not suspect a thing for years, making it impossible for her to report the abuse or seek help. This delay between the crime and its discovery creates a significant challenge for legal authorities in gathering timely evidence, prosecuting offenders, and offering justice to victims.

Furthermore, the case exposed how poorly the law dealt with issues of consent in situations where a victim is unconscious or incapacitated. While laws in France, like in many other countries, acknowledge that an unconscious person cannot give consent, the legal processes surrounding these cases often fail to reflect the seriousness of drug-facilitated rape. In Gisèle's situation, the evidence of thousands of images and videos was overwhelming, but had those records not existed, the likelihood of prosecuting Dominique and the other perpetrators would have been slim. This points to the broader issue of how reliant sexual abuse cases are on physical evidence, even when the crime itself denies the victim the capacity to remember or report the abuse.

The privacy rights of victims also became a focal point in the legal discussion surrounding this case. Dominique's meticulous recording of his wife's abuse without her knowledge raised urgent questions about the adequacy of privacy laws in France. How could someone secretly film a person for years in the privacy of their own home and share those recordings online, without any alarm bells being raised? The answer lies in the fact that current privacy laws were insufficiently robust to prevent such violations. While laws exist to punish individuals who distribute explicit material without consent, the loopholes that allowed Dominique to operate unnoticed for so long are indicative of how outdated and ineffectual those protections can be.

The case also raised questions about the role of digital platforms and their responsibility in preventing the distribution of such material. Dominique shared the recordings with others, and this digital footprint revealed the ease with which explicit and non-consensual content can be spread online. The legal framework surrounding digital crimes, especially those involving sexual abuse, is still catching up to the technological reality. Gisèle's case brought these issues to the forefront, demanding stricter regulations, more accountability for digital platforms, and stronger legal protections for victims of online exploitation.

Ultimately, Gisèle's case did more than reveal individual acts of horror; it highlighted the ways in which the law failed to foresee, prevent, or address the full scope of those horrors. The gaps in the legal system allowed Dominique Pélicot to carry out his abuse without consequence for years, while his wife remained oblivious to the violations she was suffering. This case forced the legal community and lawmakers to confront these gaps head-on, sparking conversations about how laws should be reformed to protect future victims from similar fates.

Public Outrage and Advocacy

The revelations of Gisèle Pélicot's abuse sent shockwaves through French society, igniting public outrage not only for the crimes themselves but for the systemic failures that allowed such atrocities to occur. As news of the case spread, it became a national conversation, bringing the issues of sexual violence, victim rights, and legal accountability to the forefront. For many, Gisèle's story became a symbol of how easily victims can be silenced or rendered invisible, even in their own homes.

One of the most immediate reactions to the case was the overwhelming sense of disbelief. How could something so horrific happen over such a long period of time without anyone noticing? How could a husband betray his wife so thoroughly, orchestrating a decade of abuse? The public outrage was palpable, and it was not just directed at Dominique Pélicot and the men who had participated in the abuse. It was also directed at the institutions that had failed to protect Gisèle and at the legal system that had, in many ways, enabled the abuse to continue unchecked.

This outrage quickly evolved into action. Advocacy groups that had long been fighting for stronger protections for victims of sexual violence saw a surge of support. Gisèle's case became a rallying point for those advocating for legal reforms, particularly around the issues of consent, drug-facilitated sexual assault, and digital privacy. Many women's rights organizations mobilized to ensure that Gisèle's story would not be forgotten and that it would lead to concrete changes in the law.

One of the key outcomes of this surge in advocacy was the rise of campaigns focused on addressing drug-facilitated sexual assault. Many of these campaigns aimed to raise awareness about how prevalent these crimes are, highlighting the fact that victims are often unaware that they have been assaulted, and are thus unable to seek help. Organizations began calling for better education on the signs of drug-facilitated crimes, as well as more stringent laws to prosecute those who use drugs to incapacitate their victims.

Gisèle's story also led to an increase in advocacy around the issue of privacy rights. Many of the campaigns that emerged in the wake of the case focused on the need for stricter laws around non-consensual recording and distribution of intimate material. The fact that Dominique was able to record his wife and share those recordings online without any immediate repercussions highlighted the need for more proactive measures to protect individuals from such violations. Advocacy groups began pushing for harsher penalties for those who distribute non-consensual recordings and for digital platforms to take more responsibility in preventing the spread of explicit content.

Public outrage also extended to calls for greater support for survivors of sexual violence. Gisèle's courage in coming forward and waving her anonymity inspired many other survivors to speak out about their own experiences. In the wake of the case, support groups and hotlines reported a spike in calls from individuals who had experienced similar violations but had been too afraid or ashamed to come forward. Gisèle's decision to step into the public eye, despite the trauma she had endured, gave hope to many survivors that their voices, too, could be heard.

Ultimately, Gisèle's story became a catalyst for change. The outrage it sparked led to real conversations about how society treats victims of sexual violence, how the legal system must evolve, and how advocacy groups can better support those who have been violated. Her case served as a stark reminder that behind every statistic is a human being, and that the fight for justice must be ongoing and relentless.

Media Coverage and Public Perception

From the moment the details of Gisèle Pélicot's case were revealed, the media played a crucial role in shaping public perception. As the story broke, newspapers, television channels, and online platforms scrambled to cover the harrowing details, each outlet presenting their own narrative of the events. The media's coverage, however, was not without its challenges. While it helped to bring Gisèle's case to light, it also exposed the complexities of reporting on such deeply personal and traumatic events.

In the initial days following Dominique's arrest, the media's focus was largely on the sensational aspects of the case: the drugging, the secret recordings, the involvement of dozens of men. Headlines were designed to shock and grab attention, often at the expense of a more nuanced understanding of the long-term impact of such crimes on victims like Gisèle. While the public's immediate reaction was one of outrage, there was also a darker undercurrent of voyeurism. Some media outlets were criticized for focusing too heavily on the explicit details of the abuse, rather than on the systemic issues that allowed it to continue for so long.

However, as the story developed, the media's approach shifted. Investigative journalists began digging deeper into the legal and social implications of the case. Reports highlighted the gaps in the legal system that had failed to protect Gisèle, the role of digital platforms in facilitating the distribution of non-consensual material, and the broader issues of consent in cases of drug-facilitated sexual assault. This more in-depth coverage helped to steer the public conversation towards meaningful discussions about reform and justice.

Public perception of the case was overwhelmingly supportive of Gisèle. As more details emerged, people were horrified not only by the actions of Dominique and the men involved but also by the way in which the legal system had failed her. The media's portrayal of Gisèle as a courageous woman who had endured unimaginable suffering helped to humanize her in the eyes of the public. Her decision to waive her anonymity further solidified her as a symbol of strength and resilience, inspiring many to advocate for stronger protections for victims.

However, the media's coverage was not without its controversies. Some critics argued that the intense public focus on Gisèle's case risked retraumatizing her by constantly revisiting the details of her abuse. Others pointed out that the sensationalism surrounding the case might overshadow the larger, systemic issues that needed to be addressed. Despite these criticisms, the media's role in bringing attention to the case cannot be understated. Without the coverage, it is likely that the legal and social reforms that followed might not have gained the same level of momentum.

Overall, the media's coverage of Gisèle Pélicot's case was a double-edged sword. It helped to raise awareness and galvanize public support, but it also highlighted the challenges of reporting on sexual violence in a way that respects the dignity of the victim while still holding perpetrators and institutions accountable. The public's reaction to the case was shaped by this coverage, and it played a critical role in driving the conversations that would ultimately lead to changes in both the legal system and societal attitudes towards sexual violence.

Chapter 7

Gisèle's Resilience – A Survivor's Journey

Rebuilding After Trauma

For Gisèle Pélicot, the journey toward recovery after the revelations of abuse was not a straightforward path. It was one filled with emotional upheavals, physical challenges, and a need to rebuild her sense of self from the ground up. The trauma she had endured was not only psychological; it was a complete betrayal of her body and her trust. The man she had once loved and shared a life with had turned her most intimate moments into a nightmare she could not escape. In the wake of these horrors, Gisèle's first task was to simply survive the emotional fallout.

The immediate aftermath of discovering the abuse was like being plunged into a deep, dark void. For weeks, Gisèle struggled to process the enormity of what had happened to her. She vacillated between disbelief, anger, and profound sadness. How could this have happened under her own roof? How could she have lived for so long without knowing the full extent of her suffering? These questions haunted her daily as she tried to make sense of the incomprehensible. The betrayal was not just physical; it was emotional and spiritual. Her marriage, her home once symbols of safety and love had been tainted beyond recognition.

One of the greatest emotional challenges for Gisèle was reclaiming her sense of identity. She had been objectified, reduced to something less than human by her abusers, and now she was faced with the monumental task of rediscovering who she was outside of that victimhood. It was difficult to see herself as anything other than a woman betrayed, violated, and exploited. The psychological toll of this identity crisis was severe. Gisèle grappled with feelings of worthlessness and shame, even though she intellectually knew she had done nothing wrong. Emotionally, the scars run deep, and they threaten to consume her sense of self-worth.

The physical challenges were also considerable. Years of being drugged and violated without her knowledge had left lasting effects on her body. There were health complications that arose from the repeated assaults, both physical and psychosomatic. Gisèle experienced chronic fatigue, unexplained pains, and difficulty sleeping symptoms that doctors attributed to the long-term stress and trauma she had endured. These physical reminders of the abuse made it even harder for her to move forward. Every ache, every sleepless night, felt like a cruel reminder of what had been done to her, making it difficult to separate her present self from the past.

In the face of these overwhelming challenges, Gisèle found herself standing at a crossroads. She could allow the trauma to define her, to consume her entirely, or she could begin the difficult work of rebuilding her life. It was not an easy choice. The path of recovery meant confronting her pain head-on, acknowledging the depth of her suffering while still finding a way to move forward. This required an immense amount of courage and resilience, qualities that Gisèle had unknowingly cultivated over the years as she endured the abuse without understanding it.

One of the first steps in her emotional recovery was accepting that she was not at fault. This was a crucial turning point for Gisèle. The shame and guilt that victims of sexual violence often carry can be crippling, and for a long time, she struggled with the feeling that she had somehow allowed this to happen. But with the help of therapists and support groups, she began to understand that the blame lay entirely with her abusers. Dominique and the men who participated in her abuse had preyed on her vulnerability, and it was their actions, not hers, that were reprehensible.

Rebuilding after trauma was not a linear process for Gisèle. There were days when she felt like she was making progress, reclaiming pieces of herself that had been lost in the darkness. But there were also days when the weight of what had happened seemed too heavy to bear. The grief would return in waves, unexpected and overwhelming. It was in these moments that Gisèle had to remind herself that healing is not about erasing the pain, but about learning to live alongside it. The scars would never fully disappear, but they could become part of a new, stronger self.

Facing the World: Becoming an Advocate

As Gisèle began to piece together her shattered life, she realized that she could not remain silent about what had happened to her. The decision to waive her anonymity was not just a personal act of courage, it was the beginning of her transformation from victim to advocate. Gisèle understood that her story, as painful as it was, had the power to inspire change, not just in the legal system but in the lives of other survivors who had suffered in silence.

Becoming an advocate for victims of sexual violence was not a role Gisèle had ever imagined for herself. Before the abuse was revealed, she had lived a quiet, private life, content with her small community and personal aspirations. But the trauma she had endured and the public's response to it pushed her into a new realm of visibility. Suddenly, Gisèle found herself at the center of a national conversation about sexual violence, consent, and justice. Her decision to speak out gave a voice to the many women and men who had experienced similar horrors but had not been able to share their stories.

Her emergence as an advocate was met with widespread support, but it also came with challenges. Stepping into the public eye meant that Gisèle had to relive her trauma repeatedly, telling her story to journalists, activists, and lawmakers. Each retelling was a painful reminder of what had been done to her, but Gisèle understood that sharing her experience was a necessary part of the healing process not just for herself, but for others. She wanted to be a beacon of hope for survivors, showing them that it was possible to reclaim their lives after abuse.

One of the most powerful aspects of Gisèle's advocacy was her ability to inspire others to come forward. In the months following her public statements, support groups and helplines reported a significant increase in calls from survivors who had previously been too afraid or ashamed to speak out. Gisèle's courage gave them the strength to confront their own experiences and seek the help they needed. Her story served as a reminder that there is no shame in being a victim of abuse, and that speaking out can be a transformative act of self-empowerment.

Gisèle's advocacy extended beyond just sharing her own story. She became actively involved in campaigns for legal reform, particularly around issues of consent and drug-facilitated sexual assault. She worked with women's rights organizations to push for stricter laws around privacy violations and the non-consensual recording of intimate moments. Gisèle also participated in awareness campaigns aimed at educating the public about the signs of sexual abuse, the dangers of drug-facilitated crimes, and the importance of supporting survivors.

Facing the world as an advocate was not easy for Gisèle. It required immense strength to stand in front of crowds, give interviews, and share her most intimate, painful experiences with strangers. But it was through this advocacy that Gisèle found a new sense of purpose. She was no longer defined by what had been done to her; instead, she became defined by what she was doing for others. Her story was no longer just a tale of victimhood—it was a story of resilience, strength, and the power of the human spirit to overcome even the most horrific circumstances.

The Long Road to Healing

Healing from trauma is not a one-time event; it is a journey, often a lifelong one, and Gisèle Pélicot's road to healing has been no different. The path she has walked since discovering the abuse has been fraught with obstacles, but it has also been filled with moments of profound personal growth and rediscovery. For Gisèle, healing has meant reclaiming her life on her own terms, learning to live with the scars of her past while building a future that is not defined by her trauma.

One of the most important steps in Gisèle's healing process was seeking professional therapy. From the outset, she knew that she could not face this journey alone. The trauma she had endured was too deep, too complex, to navigate without help.

Therapy provided her with a safe space to explore her feelings, confront her pain, and begin the process of rebuilding her sense of self. With the guidance of skilled therapists, Gisèle was able to unpack the layers of betrayal and violation she had experienced, slowly working through the emotions that had threatened to overwhelm her in the aftermath of the revelations.

Therapy was not just about talking, though that was an important part of it. It was also about learning practical coping mechanisms for dealing with the anxiety, depression, and post-traumatic stress disorder (PTSD) that often accompanied her memories of the abuse. Gisèle's therapists introduced her to mindfulness techniques, grounding exercises, and other tools that helped her regain control over her thoughts and emotions. These techniques became invaluable in her daily life, allowing her to manage the flashbacks and panic attacks that would sometimes surface without warning.

In addition to therapy, Gisèle found strength in support groups. Surrounding herself with other survivors of sexual violence helped her realize that she was not alone in her struggle. These groups provided her with a sense of community, a place where she could share her experiences without fear of judgment. The women (and men) she met in these groups became a source of inspiration for her. Each of them had endured their own unique traumas, and yet they were all united by the common goal of healing and reclaiming their lives.

Support systems extended beyond the therapy room and support groups. Gisèle also leaned heavily on her friends and family during this time. While her relationship with her family had been strained by the revelations of the abuse, particularly with those who had known Dominique and had once trusted him, they rallied around her as she began her journey toward healing. Their unwavering love and support became a crucial part of her recovery, reminding her that she still had people in her life who cared deeply for her well-being.

Another significant step in Gisèle's healing was her decision to rebuild her physical health. The years of drug-facilitated abuse had taken a toll on her body, leaving her with lingering health issues. Gisèle took control of her physical recovery by working with doctors and nutritionists to improve her overall well-being. She began exercising regularly, focusing on activities like yoga and walking, which helped her reconnect with her body in a positive way. Slowly, she began to regain a sense of physical strength that had been stolen from her during the years of abuse.

Healing is never a straight path, and Gisèle's journey has had its setbacks. There are still days when the weight of what she has endured feels unbearable. But through therapy, support systems, and her own inner resilience, she has learned to navigate those dark moments. She has learned that healing is not about erasing the past, it is about learning to live with it, to carry the scars without letting them define her.

For Gisèle, the long road to healing continues. It is a journey marked by both pain and triumph, sorrow and hope. But each day that she chooses to move forward, each step she takes toward reclaiming her life, is a victory. In the end, Gisèle's story is not just about surviving trauma, it is about the resilience of the human spirit, the power of healing, and the ability to rise from the ashes of suffering to create a new, stronger self.

Chapter 8

Current Challenges and Her Role Today

The Ongoing Legal Process

Though Dominique Pélicot's arrest marked the beginning of a significant legal battle, the process of achieving full justice has been slow and fraught with complexity. The legal journey is still ongoing, with numerous appeals, counterclaims, and strategic delays on the part of Dominique and his legal team. These efforts have not only prolonged the legal process but have also kept Gisèle tied to the trauma, preventing her from fully closing this painful chapter of her life.

As of today, Dominique Pélicot remains incarcerated, but his defense team has been relentless in seeking to overturn or reduce the charges against him. His lawyers have argued that certain pieces of evidence were obtained without proper legal procedure, citing technicalities related to the seizure of digital devices during the initial investigation. These attempts to discredit the overwhelming evidence against him have been met with fierce opposition from prosecutors, who maintain that the evidence, including thousands of images and videos documenting the abuse, speaks for itself.

In addition to challenging the evidence, Dominique's defense has also attempted to minimize his role in the abuse, claiming that the other men involved were more culpable and that his own participation was limited. This narrative has been met with widespread condemnation, as it blatantly disregards the fact that Dominique was the orchestrator of the entire operation. He was the one who drugged his wife, invited other men to assault her, and documented the abuse for his own sick pleasure. The legal team representing Gisèle and the prosecution have remained steadfast in their pursuit of justice, fighting to ensure that Dominique faces the full consequences of his actions.

The involvement of the other men has also complicated the legal process. Many of these men have been brought to trial, but their cases are being handled individually, which means that the legal proceedings are drawn out over months and years. Some of these men have attempted to downplay their involvement, claiming ignorance of Gisèle's drugged state, but the evidence provided by the videos has been damning. Each new trial forces Gisèle to relive her trauma, as the details of her abuse are revisited time and time again in court.

For Gisèle, the ongoing nature of the legal battle is exhausting. Every new appeal, every attempt by Dominique to avoid accountability, feels like another violation—a refusal to acknowledge the pain he has caused. The legal system, slow and methodical by nature, can often feel like it is working against victims rather than for them. Gisèle's desire for closure is constantly thwarted by the bureaucratic processes and legal loopholes that Dominique's defense team exploits.

However, despite the emotional toll of these delays, Gisèle remains resolute in her pursuit of justice. She has been unwavering in her commitment to see Dominique and the other men held fully accountable for their actions. The strength she shows in the face of these continued legal battles is a testament to her resilience. Even as Dominique's defense tries to wear her down with delays and technicalities, Gisèle continues to fight for justice, not just for herself but for all victims of sexual abuse who have been failed by the system.

The ongoing legal process serves as a reminder of how difficult it can be for survivors to find justice, even when the evidence is overwhelmingly in their favour. For Gisèle, every court appearance, every hearing, is another step toward reclaiming her life from the horrors that were inflicted upon her. She knows that the road to justice is long, but she is determined to see it through, no matter how many obstacles Dominique and his legal team try to place in her way.

Gisèle's Present-Day Life

In the wake of the revelations about her abuse, Gisèle Pélicot's life has been irreversibly changed. The years since the discovery have been filled with emotional turbulence, media attention, and the struggle to regain a sense of normalcy. While Gisèle has made significant strides in her healing journey, her daily life is still marked by the weight of her past, the ongoing legal battles, and the public scrutiny that accompanies being at the center of such a high-profile case.

Gisèle's present-day life is a delicate balance between her private healing and her public role as a survivor and advocate. On a personal level, she continues to work through the emotional and psychological impact of the abuse. Therapy remains an essential part of her routine, providing her with the support and guidance she needs to navigate the complexities of her trauma. While she has come a long way since the initial shock of the revelations, there are still days when the memories of what happened threaten to overwhelm her. Flashbacks, nightmares, and bouts of anxiety are not uncommon, but Gisèle has developed coping mechanisms that allow her to manage these symptoms and continue moving forward.

Her physical health, too, has been a priority. The years of drug-facilitated abuse left her with lingering health issues, and she remains vigilant about her physical well-being. Regular check-ups, a healthy diet, and exercise have become part of her routine, not only to maintain her physical health but also as a way of reclaiming control over her body. Yoga and meditation have been particularly helpful in allowing Gisèle to reconnect with herself in a positive, healing way, providing moments of peace amidst the ongoing chaos of the legal process and public attention.

Privacy, however, remains one of the most significant challenges in Gisèle's life today. Since she waived her anonymity to bring attention to her case and advocate for other victims, she has been thrust into the public eye in a way that she could never have anticipated. While this decision has allowed her to inspire others and push for meaningful change, it has also come at a personal cost. The media attention has made it difficult for her to lead a fully private life. Every appearance in court, every new development in the case, is reported on by the press, and while much of the coverage is sympathetic, the constant attention can feel invasive.

Public appearances, though empowering, are also emotionally taxing. Gisèle has become a symbol of resilience, and while she is proud of the role she plays in advocating for other survivors, it can be difficult to live up to the expectations placed upon her. Each public speech or interview requires her to relive her trauma, to speak openly about the darkest moments of her life in order to shed light on the experiences of other survivors. This vulnerability, though powerful, comes at a personal cost. After each appearance, Gisèle often feels drained, needing time to retreat and recover from the emotional intensity of sharing her story with the world.

Despite these challenges, Gisèle continues to find moments of joy and peace in her daily life. She has reconnected with old friends, repaired relationships with family members, and found solace in simple pleasures reading, cooking, and spending time in nature. While her life will never be the same as it was before the abuse was uncovered, she is slowly building a new sense of normalcy, one that allows her to embrace the future while acknowledging the scars of her past.

Challenges of Advocacy

While Gisèle Pélicot's role as an advocate for survivors of sexual violence has been a source of strength and purpose, it has also presented its own set of challenges. In stepping into the spotlight, Gisèle has had to confront not only her own trauma but also the broader societal attitudes towards sexual violence, victimhood, and justice. As much as her story has inspired others, it has also exposed the many obstacles that survivors face when trying to bring attention to their experiences.

One of the biggest challenges Gisèle has faced as an advocate is the stigma that still surrounds sexual violence. While public attitudes are slowly changing, many survivors continue to be met with skepticism, blame, or outright disbelief when they come forward with their stories. Gisèle's case, though well-documented and supported by irrefutable evidence, was no exception to this. There were those who questioned her decision to waive her anonymity, who suggested that she was seeking attention or profit from her trauma. These criticisms, though hurtful, have not deterred Gisèle from continuing her advocacy work, but they are a constant reminder of the uphill battle that survivors face in a society that often blames victims instead of holding perpetrators accountable.

Another challenge has been navigating the legal and bureaucratic hurdles that come with advocacy. Gisèle has become involved in several campaigns aimed at reforming laws related to sexual violence, consent, and digital privacy, but the process of pushing for legal change is slow and frustrating. While her story has garnered widespread attention, translating that attention into concrete policy changes has been a difficult and often discouraging task. Lawmakers, though sympathetic, are often bound by the complexities of the legal system, and progress can feel excruciatingly slow. Gisèle has had to learn patience, understanding that real change takes time, but it has not been easy to reconcile the urgency of her cause with the often glacial pace of legal reform.

The emotional toll of advocacy has also been significant. Each time Gisèle speaks publicly about her experiences, she is forced to revisit the trauma of her past. While she has developed coping mechanisms to manage this, the emotional burden of constantly reliving her story can be overwhelming. There are times when she feels as though she is defined solely by her trauma, as though the world only sees her as a victim, not as a whole person with a life beyond the abuse. Balancing her personal healing with her public role has been a delicate and ongoing challenge.

Despite these obstacles, Gisèle remains committed to her advocacy work. She knows that her voice, though often tired and strained from the weight of her experiences, is a powerful tool for change. Her story has inspired countless survivors to come forward, and she has seen firsthand the impact that her advocacy can have on both individual lives and broader societal conversations about sexual violence. Gisèle's résilience, both as a survivor and as an advocate, continues to drive her forward, even in the face of the many challenges she faces.

In many ways, Gisèle's journey as an advocate mirrors her personal journey of healing. It is not a straight path, and it is filled with setbacks, frustrations, and emotional pain. But it is also a path of growth, empowerment, and hope. Each obstacle she overcomes, whether in her personal life or in her advocacy work, is a testament to her strength and her unwavering commitment to helping other survivors find their voices. Gisèle's story is not just about surviving trauma—it is about transforming that trauma into a force for change, and in doing so, she has become a beacon of hope for countless others.

Chapter 9

The Global Impact of Gisèle Pélicot's Story

Lessons Learned from Gisèle's Case

The story of Gisèle Pélicot is one that has resonated across the globe, not just because of the harrowing nature of her experience, but because of what it reveals about victimhood, resilience, and the systems meant to protect the vulnerable. Gisèle's journey from victim to advocate has taught the world important lessons about how we view and treat survivors of sexual violence, and how much further we must go in addressing the failures of legal and societal structures that are supposed to offer protection.

One of the most striking lessons from Gisèle's case is the profound resilience that survivors of sexual violence often demonstrate. Despite the unimaginable betrayal and years of abuse, Gisèle has managed to reclaim her life and use her story as a vehicle for change. Her decision to waive her anonymity, while emotionally challenging, was a brave and powerful act that turned her from an invisible victim into a visible and vocal advocate. This act of defiance in the face of overwhelming trauma has shown the world that survivors, no matter how broken they may feel, can find strength within themselves to rise and fight for justice.

Beyond personal resilience, Gisèle's case has also highlighted the importance of community and societal support for victims of abuse. Her journey has taught us that while individual strength is crucial, it is not enough. Survivors need support systems—whether through therapy, family, friends, or community organizations to help them navigate the complex emotional and psychological toll of trauma. Gisèle's recovery and advocacy work have underscored the value of these networks, and her story has inspired many organizations to strengthen their efforts in providing safe spaces for victims to come forward and begin their healing process.

Perhaps one of the most significant lessons from Gisèle's case is the critical need for legal reform. The fact that Dominique Pélicot was able to abuse his wife for nearly a decade without detection reveals serious gaps in the legal and judicial systems meant to protect victims. Gisèle's case has brought to light the inadequacies of laws surrounding sexual violence, consent, and digital privacy. In particular, it has sparked discussions around how the law should handle cases of drug-facilitated sexual assault, where the victim is often unaware of the abuse for long periods of time.

Legal reforms are now being discussed in France and other parts of the world, driven in large part by the lessons learned from Gisèle's case. Lawmakers are considering stricter penalties for those who use drugs to incapacitate victims, as well as stronger privacy laws to prevent the non-consensual recording and distribution of intimate images. Additionally, there is a growing movement to address the often slow and cumbersome nature of the legal process in cases involving sexual violence. The delays and appeals that have plagued Gisèle's case have shown the world that justice delayed is indeed justice denied, and reforms are needed to ensure that victims do not have to wait years to see their abusers brought to justice.

The Broader Conversation on Sexual Violence

Gisèle Pélicot's story is not an isolated incident; rather, it is part of a broader global conversation on sexual violence, consent, and victim empowerment. Her case has become a touchstone for discussions around how society responds to sexual abuse, and it has contributed to the ongoing dialogue about what justice for survivors truly looks like. In this way, Gisèle's experience fits into a larger movement that seeks to challenge and dismantle the societal norms that allow sexual violence to persist.

At the heart of this broader conversation is the issue of consent. Gisèle's case has drawn attention to the complexities of consent, particularly in situations where a victim is incapacitated by drugs or alcohol. Her story has highlighted the urgent need for clearer laws and societal understanding of what constitutes consent, especially in cases where the victim is not conscious or able to give explicit permission. This has resonated globally, as many other countries grapple with similar legal ambiguities around consent and how it is defined in the context of sexual violence.

Gisèle's case also fits into a larger global narrative of victim empowerment. Across the world, survivors of sexual violence are beginning to find their voices, challenging the stigma and shame that have long kept them silent. Movements like #MeToo and Time's Up have provided platforms for survivors to share their stories, and Gisèle's decision to speak out publicly aligns with this growing wave of victim empowerment. Her story, like so many others, is helping to shift the narrative from one of silence and victim-blaming to one of courage and accountability.

The global conversation on sexual violence has also been shaped by high-profile cases that bear similarities to Gisèle's. For instance, the case of Bill Cosby in the United States, where numerous women came forward to accuse the comedian of drugging and sexually assaulting them, echoes many of the elements of Gisèle's story. Both cases involve powerful men using drugs to incapacitate their victims, and both have sparked widespread public outrage and calls for legal reform. Similarly, the case of Harvey Weinstein, whose predatory behavior was exposed through the courage of his victims, has further fueled the global conversation on consent, power dynamics, and the need for systemic change.

Gisèle's case stands as a reminder that sexual violence is not confined to one culture, country, or social class it is a global issue that affects millions of people every year. Her story has contributed to a broader understanding of the ways in which power and control are wielded in cases of sexual abuse, and it has underscored the importance of empowering victims to take control of their narratives.

Moreover, Gisèle's experience has highlighted the role of technology in modern sexual violence. The use of digital devices to record and distribute images of her abuse adds a layer of complexity to the conversation, one that is increasingly relevant in an age where technology is often used as a tool of exploitation. Gisèle's case has forced society to confront the ways in which technology can be weaponized against victims, and it has sparked important discussions around the need for stronger digital privacy laws and regulations.

In the broader context of global sexual violence, Gisèle Pélicot's story is a powerful example of both the pervasiveness of abuse and the resilience of survivors. Her case has helped to push the global conversation forward, challenging outdated norms and advocating for a more just and compassionate world for survivors of sexual violence.

Changing Attitudes and Policies

Gisèle Pélicot's case has had a profound impact on French society, particularly in terms of changing attitudes toward sexual violence, consent, and privacy laws. In the wake of her story, there has been a significant shift in public consciousness around these issues, leading to increased calls for policy changes and legal reforms that better protect victims and hold perpetrators accountable.

One of the most noticeable changes in attitudes has been around the issue of consent. Before Gisèle's case came to light, discussions about consent often revolved around explicit verbal agreement. However, her story has underscored the need for a more nuanced understanding of consent, especially in cases where the victim is incapacitated. The fact that Dominique Pélicot was able to drug his wife and allow others to assault her without her knowledge has forced society to rethink what it means to give or withhold consent. This has led to public pressure on lawmakers to enact stricter laws that protect victims of drug-facilitated sexual violence and ensure that perpetrators face appropriate consequences.

In response to this public outcry, French lawmakers have begun to explore new legislation that would close some of the legal loopholes that allowed Dominique to carry out his abuse for so long. Among the proposed changes are harsher penalties for individuals who use drugs to incapacitate their victims and stronger protections for victims of digital exploitation. Gisèle's case has also prompted discussions about the need for faster legal proceedings in cases of sexual violence, as the slow pace of the legal process has been a source of frustration for many survivors seeking justice.

The impact of Gisèle's case has also been felt in the realm of privacy laws. Dominique's ability to record and distribute videos of his wife's abuse without her knowledge has shone a spotlight on the inadequacies of current privacy protections. In response, there has been a growing movement to strengthen privacy laws, particularly around the non-consensual recording and sharing of intimate images. These efforts have been bolstered by advocacy groups that have used Gisèle's case as a rallying point to push for more comprehensive legislation that protects victims from digital exploitation.

Gisèle's case has also contributed to a broader cultural shift in how sexual violence is discussed and understood in France. Her story has helped to break down some of the stigma that has historically surrounded survivors of sexual abuse, encouraging more open and honest conversations about the realities of victimhood. Public attitudes toward survivors have become more compassionate, and there is a growing recognition that the burden of shame should never fall on the victim but rather on the perpetrator.

This cultural shift is particularly important in the context of women's rights in France. Gisèle's case has been a catalyst for renewed discussions about gender-based violence and the systemic inequalities that often prevent women from seeking or receiving justice. The widespread support that Gisèle has received from women's rights organizations has helped to amplify calls for legal reforms and has strengthened the movement for gender equality in the country.

Ultimately, the impact of Gisèle Pélicot's story on French society and beyond cannot be overstated. Her bravery in coming forward, despite the trauma she endured, has sparked important conversations and policy changes that will benefit survivors of sexual violence for years to come. The legal reforms that are now being discussed, the shifts in public attitudes toward consent and privacy, and the increased support for women's rights are all part of Gisèle's enduring legacy. Her story is not just one of suffering, it is a story of resilience, advocacy, and change.

Conclusion

The Road Ahead - Gisèle Pélicot's Legacy

Ongoing Challenges in French Legal Reform

Gisèle Pélicot's case has ignited widespread debates about the need for more comprehensive legal protections for victims of sexual assault in France. Despite the global attention her story has received, the journey toward significant legal reform remains slow, as systemic issues and bureaucratic hurdles continue to impede meaningful progress. Nevertheless, her story has been a catalyst for ongoing discussions, pushing lawmakers, advocacy groups, and the public to confront the legal inadequacies that her case exposed.

One of the primary challenges in French legal reform has been the need for a clearer definition of consent in situations involving incapacitated victims. Gisèle's case starkly illustrated the loopholes in the existing legal framework, where perpetrators who use drugs to incapacitate their victims can often exploit ambiguities in the law. Dominique Pélicot's ability to drug his wife and enable her assault for nearly a decade without detection highlights a critical gap in how the law treats cases of drug-facilitated sexual assault. While consent laws in France acknowledge that an unconscious person cannot give consent, the nuances of drug-facilitated crimes where victims may have no memory of the events pose complex legal challenges.

In response to the public outcry over Gisèle's case, lawmakers have begun to discuss reforms that would establish stricter penalties for those who use drugs or alcohol to incapacitate victims, as well as enhanced protections for those who may not immediately realize they have been assaulted. This includes proposed changes to the statute of limitations in sexual assault cases, giving victims more time to come forward once they become aware of the abuse. Gisèle's story has been a powerful reminder that many survivors of sexual violence do not have the luxury of immediate awareness or the capacity to report the crime while it is happening. These reforms, if passed, would represent a significant step forward in ensuring that victims of drug-facilitated sexual assault receive the justice they deserve.

Another area where Gisèle's story continues to influence legal reform is in the realm of privacy laws. The recordings of her abuse, made without her knowledge or consent, revealed serious shortcomings in French privacy protections. Dominique's ability to document the abuse and share those recordings with others without immediate legal repercussions raised alarm about the state of digital privacy laws. In today's technologically advanced world, where it is easier than ever to capture and distribute intimate images without consent, Gisèle's case has underscored the urgent need for stronger laws around non-consensual recording and distribution.

Advocacy groups have used her case to push for more stringent penalties for those who engage in "revenge porn" or other forms of digital exploitation. They argue that the law needs to evolve to protect victims from not just the physical aspects of sexual violence but also the digital violations that often accompany it. The proposed legal reforms would criminalize the act of recording and distributing intimate content without consent, with harsher sentences for those who use such material to exploit or humiliate their victims.

However, the road to legal reform in France is long, and resistance from some sectors remains. Conservative lawmakers and organizations have raised concerns about how these reforms might affect due process or unintentionally criminalize consensual behavior. Additionally, the slow pace of legislative change has been a source of frustration for many, including survivors like Gisèle, who continue to face the consequences of inadequate legal protections.

Despite these challenges, Gisèle's case has created a ripple effect that has brought the issue of legal reform for victims of sexual assault to the forefront of public consciousness. Her story continues to serve as a powerful example of why the legal system must evolve to better protect the vulnerable, and while the battle for meaningful reform is far from over, her influence on these discussions will undoubtedly endure.

The Legacy of Courage

Gisèle Pélicot's legacy is one defined by extraordinary courage, resilience, and an unwavering commitment to justice. Her story, once hidden in the shadows of betrayal and abuse, has become a symbol of strength for victims of sexual violence around the world. What began as a private nightmare has transformed into a public narrative of survival, advocacy, and hope. Gisèle's courage in coming forward, despite the emotional and psychological toll of her trauma, has redefined what it means to be a survivor and has given a voice to those who have long been silenced.

Her decision to waive her anonymity was not just a personal act of bravery, it was a turning point in the broader conversation about sexual violence. In revealing her identity and sharing her story with the world, Gisèle challenged the pervasive stigma that surrounds victims of abuse. She refused to be defined by what had been done to her, instead choosing to take control of her narrative and use her platform to advocate for others who had experienced similar atrocities. Her courage in the face of such overwhelming pain has inspired countless others to step forward and seek justice, many for the first time in their lives.

Gisèle's legacy also extends beyond her personal story. She has become a symbol of resilience for survivors of all kinds, demonstrating that it is possible to rebuild one's life after profound trauma. Her journey is a testament to the human capacity for healing and transformation, even when the road ahead seems impossible. Through her advocacy work, Gisèle has shown that while the scars of abuse may never fully fade, they do not have to define a person's future. Her strength serves as a beacon of hope for those who are still trapped in their own darkness, offering them the possibility of a brighter, more empowered future.

For future generations, Gisèle's legacy will be one of inspiration and action. Her story will continue to be a powerful reminder that courage is not the absence of fear, but the ability to move forward in spite of it. In a world where many still remain silent about their experiences of abuse, Gisèle's voice will resonate as a call to action for individuals to speak out, for communities to support survivors, and for governments to enact the laws needed to protect the most vulnerable among us.

Her advocacy work has already had a profound impact on how sexual violence is discussed and addressed in France and beyond. Through her public appearances, interviews, and collaboration with women's rights organizations, Gisèle has brought attention to the systemic failures that allowed her abuse to go unnoticed for so long. She has played a key role in shifting societal attitudes toward victims of sexual violence, encouraging greater empathy, understanding, and support for those who have been harmed.

Gisèle's legacy as a symbol of courage will continue to inspire future generations to challenge the systems that perpetuate abuse and to fight for justice in the face of overwhelming odds. Her story is one of resilience, but it is also a story of action of a woman who refused to be silenced and who used her voice to advocate for change. In this way, her legacy will live on, not just in the legal reforms that her case has inspired, but in the hearts and minds of those who have been touched by her story.

Gisèle's Message to the World

Gisèle Pélicot's message to the world is one of profound empathy, resilience, and a relentless pursuit of justice. For victims of abuse, her words are a source of hope and validation, reminding them that they are not alone and that their stories deserve to be heard. To society, she issues a challenge: to stand up for the most vulnerable, to believe survivors, and to ensure that justice is not just an abstract ideal but a tangible reality for all. And to those in positions of power, her message is clear: the time for change is now.

To victims of abuse, Gisèle's message is one of solidarity and understanding. She knows all too well the pain of silence, the weight of shame, and the fear of coming forward. But she also knows the power of speaking out. "You are not defined by what happened to you," she often says in her public addresses. "You are more than your trauma, more than your pain. You have a voice, and that voice matters." Gisèle's message to survivors is simple but profound: healing is possible, even in the face of unimaginable suffering. She encourages survivors to seek support, to find their community, and to remember that their worth is not diminished by what they have endured.

For society, Gisèle's message is a call to action. She urges people to confront the cultural norms that allow abuse to flourish in silence. "We must create a world where survivors are believed, where their stories are taken seriously, and where they are given the support they need to heal," she has said in numerous interviews. Gisèle's advocacy has consistently highlighted the importance of education, awareness, and empathy in changing societal attitudes toward sexual violence. She challenges communities to stand with survivors, to break the cycle of silence, and to hold perpetrators accountable. Her message to society is one of collective responsibility: we all have a role to play in dismantling the structures that enable abuse and in building a culture of safety and respect.

To those in power lawmakers, policymakers, and judicial authorities, Gisèle's message is one of urgency. Her case has exposed the deep flaws in the legal and social systems that are supposed to protect victims, and she has been vocal about the need for reform. "The law failed me," she has said, "and it continues to fail too many others." Her message to those in power is a demand for change stronger laws, swifter justice, and more comprehensive protections for victims of sexual violence. She advocates for the closing of legal loopholes that allow perpetrators to evade accountability and for the creation of laws that address the unique challenges faced by survivors of drug-facilitated assault.

Gisèle's message is also a personal one: a plea for compassion and understanding from those who may never fully understand the depth of her trauma. "I don't expect the world to feel my pain," she once said, "but I do expect the world to care." Her life story is a powerful reminder that behind every statistic is a human being, someone who deserves dignity, justice, and the chance to rebuild their life. Through her words, Gisèle calls on society to listen, to care, and to act. Her message is a testament to the resilience of the human spirit and the enduring power of justice.

Printed in Great Britain
by Amazon